Creative Kids
FOURTH GRADE
Brain Teasers

Editors: Ina Massler Levin, M.A. and Michael H. Levin, M.A.
Illustrator: Howard Chaney
Cover Art: Chris Macabitas

Table of Contents

Things with Numbers 2
All Alike. 3
Word Pairs 4
Which Side Are You On? 5
Car Word Parts. 6
Word Pictures 7
Which One Does Not Belong?. 8
Theodore 9
Birthday Parties. 10
What's the Question? 11
Categorizing 12
How Is Your Memory? 13
What's the Message? 14
Rhyming Word Pairs 15
How Many?. 16
Word Stair Puzzle 17
Double' Em. 18
Those Famous Threes 19
Backward and Forward 20
Compound Words 21
Antonyms, Synonyms, and
Homophones. 22
More Antonyms, Synonyms, and
Homophones. 23
Palindromes 24
Proverbs 25
Similes 26
Country and City Match. 27
Analogies 28
Compound Words 29
Answer Key. 30

Introduction

Turn spare minutes into learning time. Share these challenging and engaging activities with your child to develop logic and reasoning skills. These brain teasers make learning fun.

Teacher Created Materials, Inc.
P.O. Box 1040
Huntington Beach, CA 92647
ISBN-1-57690-258-7

Made in U.S.A.

Things with Numbers

Brainstorm! Think of as many ways as you can in which people use numbers. Write them below. For example, a calendar has numbers.

1. _____
2. _____
3. _____
4. _____
5. _____
6. _____
7. _____
8. _____
9. _____
10. _____
11. _____
12. _____
13. _____
14. _____
15. _____
16. _____
17. _____
18. _____
19. _____
20. _____

All Alike

Read the words on each line. Explain how they are alike. An example has been done for you.

north, south, east = cardinal directions

1. jazz, tap, ballet _____

2. tennis, soccer, basketball _____

3. lily, daffodil, gardenia _____

4. tiger, lion, jaguar _____

5. cookies, candy, ice cream _____

6. wrench, drill, hammer _____

7. mad, silly, grumpy _____

8. diamond, ruby, amethyst _____

9. milk, butter, cheese _____

10. single, alone, individual _____

11. orange, tennis ball, marble _____

12. plane, blimp, helicopter _____

13. pencil, pen, marker _____

14. Helena, Hillary, Heather_____

15. Hubbard, zucchini, acorn_____

Word Pairs

Write the missing half of each pair.

1. _____ and puff

2. _____ and feather

3. _____ and dogs

4. _____ and cranny

5. _____ and thin

6. _____ and match

7. _____ and nail

8. _____ and sugar

9. _____ and dandy

10. _____ and forth

11. _____ and holler

12. _____ and stones

13. _____ and down

14. _____ and cents

15. _____ and cream

16. _____ and order

17. _____ and fall

18. _____ and peace

19. _____ and out

20. _____ and white

21. _____ and proper

22. _____ and soul

23. _____ and satin

24. _____ and ladder

25. _____ and paper

Which Side Are You On?

All the phrases in the sentences below can be filled in with words that contain the word *side*. Fill in the blanks to find out which side you are on.

1. The referee called a s___ ___ ___   o___t in volleyball.

2. My sweater was turned i___ ___ ___ ___ ___   ___ut.

3. It was raining ___ ___ts___ ___e.

4. A square is a f___ ___r — s___ ___e___ figure.

5. The car was b___ ___ ___ds___ ___e___ in the accident.

6. We went u___s___d___   d___w___ on the roller coaster.

7. I left my book on the b___d___i___e table.

8. We pulled off on the ___ ___ft   s___de of the road.

9. He stood on my r___ght   ___i___e.

10. I like my eggs cooked s___nn___—si ___ ___   ___p.

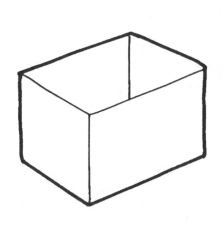

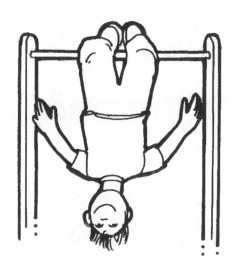

Car Word Parts

Each word or phrase below is a clue for a word that contains the word *car*. An example has been done for you.

baby buggy = carriage

1. box _____

2. red bird _____

3. chewy candy _____

4. button-up sweater _____

5. merry-go-round _____

6. animated films _____

7. wagon _____

8. flower _____

9. floor covering _____

10. orange vegetable _____

11. cut up _____

12. meat-eating animal _____

13. fair _____

14. unit of weight for gems _____

15. a deck of 52 _____

Word Pictures

Can you figure out what these word pictures are saying?

1. _____

shame
you

2. _____

3. _____

Dance
Dance   Dance
Dance

4. _____

5. _____

Hang **ON**

6. _____

7. _____

8. _____

Which One Does Not Belong?

In each line below, one of the four words does not belong with the other three. Circle the one that does not fit. Explain what the others have in common. An example has been done for you.

relish, (hot dogs,) mustard, ketchup = condiments

1. October, November, December, June _____

2. boot, shoe, glove, slipper_____

3. notebook, pencil, pen, crayon _____

4. king, queen, prince, page _____

5. Bob, Robert, Rich, Robby _____

6. ebony, mahogany, carnation, cherry _____

7. chocolate chip, ginger snap, layer cake, animal cookie _____

8. girl, lass, nephew, woman _____

9. tape recorder, television, telephone, microphone _____

10. table, chair, sofa, flower_____

11. cantaloupe, casaba, grapefruit, watermelon _____

12. strange, thud, cry, hiss_____

13. cougar, jaguar, lion, elephant_____

14. hammer, screwdriver, drill, lightbulb_____

15. exclamation mark, question mark, colon, period _____

Theodore

Mr. Martin has three boys in his science class who each go by a variation of the name Theodore. From the statements below, discover each boy's full name and age. Mark the correct boxes with an X.

1. Agee is younger than Dalton but older than Chin.

2. Ted is not the youngest or the oldest.

3. Theodore's last name is Chin.

4. None of the boys is the same age.

	Agee	Chin	Dalton	8	9	10
Ted						
Theodore						
Teddy						

Birthday Parties

Eight children in one neighborhood will turn ten this year. From the clues below, determine the month of each child's birthday. Mark the correct boxes with an **X**.

	January 1	February 21	March 25	April 7	May 7	July 15	August 3	October 30
Victor								
Mary								
Marco								
Christina								
Vicky								
Mike								
Danielle								
Peter								

1. Everyone celebrates on Mary's birthday.

2. Danielle's birthday is before Mike's but after Marco's and Victor's.

3. Victor's birthday is exactly one month after Marco's.

4. Christina's birthday is during a winter month.

5. Vicky's birthday comes after Danielle's but before Mike's.

What's the Question?

Write a question for each of the following answers.

1. Question: _____

   Answer: The Bible

2. Question: _____

   Answer: 1776

3. Question: _____

   Answer: Christopher Columbus

4. Question: _____

   Answer: 144

5. Question: _____

   Answer: Amadeus Mozart

6. Question: _____

   Answer: a rectangle

7. Question: _____

   Answer: Hawaii

8. Question: _____

   Answer: six

9. Question: _____

   Answer: no

10. Question: _____

    Answer: Saturn

11. Question: _____

    Answer: a shovel

12. Question: _____

    Answer: the Eiffel Tower

Categorizing

In the word box below are 42 words, each of which belongs in one of the six categories—wood, metals, water, space, colors, and furniture. Place each of the words under the correct category. For example, **bay** would belong in the water category. Seven words belong under each category.

- bay
- Mars
- rocket
- creek
- sea
- lamp
- lumber
- tin
- mirror
- oak
- lake
- ocean
- dresser
- tan
- scarlet
- bronze
- red
- moon
- chest
- pond
- orbit
- board
- cabinet
- couch
- steel
- blue
- green
- river
- beige
- copper
- iron
- forest
- nail
- rocker
- walnut
- astronaut
- chartreuse
- aluminum
- weightless
- countdown
- pencil
- maple

Wood

_____
_____
_____
_____
_____
_____
_____

Metals

_____
_____
_____
_____
_____
_____
_____

Water

_____
_____
_____
_____
_____
_____
_____

Space

_____
_____
_____
_____
_____
_____
_____

Colors

_____
_____
_____
_____
_____
_____
_____

Furniture

_____
_____
_____
_____
_____
_____
_____

How Is Your Memory?

Study the picture for three minutes. Then, put it out of sight. On another sheet of paper, list as many items from the picture as you can remember.

What's the Message?

A word related to each of the famous people on this page can be found by using the phone code in each sentence. The letters on the phone that correspond to the numbers on the phone create the code. Use a real phone or the picture of the key pad on this page.

1. Flying made Charles Lindbergh a famous __ __ __ __ __ __ __.
   2 8 4 – 2 8 6 7

2. Elizabeth is the queen of __ __ __ __ __ __ __.
   3 6 4 – 5 2 6 3

3. Abraham Lincoln shows up on __ __ __ __ __ __ __.
   7 3 6 – 6 4 3 7

4. Dwight Eisenhower was a military __ __ __ __ __ __ __.
   4 3 6 – 3 7 2 5

5. Nancy Kerrigan is known for her __ __ __ __ __ __ __ in the Olympics.
   7 5 2 – 8 4 6 4

6. Patrick Henry believed in __ __ __ __ __ __ __.
   5 4 2 – 3 7 8 9

7. Charlie Brown is a character in __ __ __ __ __ __ __.
   7 3 2 – 6 8 8 7

8. Helen Keller read using __ __ __ __ __ __ __.
   2 7 2 – 4 5 5 3

9. Junípero Serra founded the __ __ __ __ __ __ __ in San Juan
   6 4 7 – 7 4 6 6
   Capistrano, California.

10. Dr. Seuss and Maurice Sendak are children's __ __ __ __ __ __ __.
    2 8 8 – 4 6 7 7

Rhyming Word Pairs

Find an adjective that rhymes with a noun so that together the two words have about the same meaning as the phrase that is given. An example has been done for you.

soaked dog = soggy doggy

1. heavy slumber _____

2. second male sibling _____

3. able Daniel _____

4. big flat boat _____

5. naked bunny _____

6. high shopping center _____

7. crazy kid _____

8. wooden lower limb _____

9. igloo _____

10. tuna dinner _____

11. consume beef _____

12. funny William _____

13. heavy feline _____

14. impolite man _____

15. extra bus money _____

16. short cry _____

17. extra points _____

18. aging green stuff _____

19. downcast father _____

20. loafing flower _____

How Many?

Answer each question with a number.

How many . . .

1. sides in an octagon? □

2. keys on a piano? □

3. sheets of paper in a ream? □

4. years in 4 score? □

5. members of the U.S. Senate? □

6. months in a year? □

7. sides on a cube? □

8. instruments in a trio? □

9. days in a leap year? □

10. consonants in the alphabet? □

11. holes on a full golf course? □

12. dozen in a gross? □

13. cards in a deck with jokers? □

14. words is a picture worth? □

15. wheels on a tricycle? □

16. inches in a foot? □

17. numbers on a telephone? □

18. original United States colonies? □

19. degrees in a right triangle? □

20. players on a soccer team on the field? □

Word Stair Puzzle

Use the clues to fill in the grid.

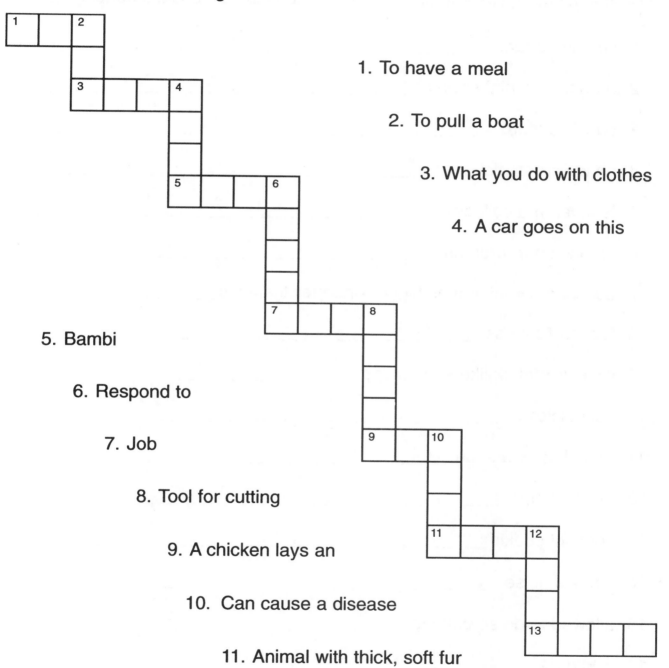

1. To have a meal

2. To pull a boat

3. What you do with clothes

4. A car goes on this

5. Bambi

6. Respond to

7. Job

8. Tool for cutting

9. A chicken lays an

10. Can cause a disease

11. Animal with thick, soft fur

12. Royalty

13. Female child

Double' Em

Use the following clues to find words that contain consecutive double letters.

1. very important _____

2. drop from a higher place _____

3. part of a word _____

4. an ice-cream flavor _____

5. teacher in a college _____

6. to take short breaths _____

7. describe something as bigger or better than it is _____

8. feeling sadness _____

9. walk with duck-like short steps _____

10. spectacles _____

11. mark left by a shoe _____

12. of little help _____

13. coconut cookie _____

14. horse's noise _____

15. allowed to do something _____

16. wild duck _____

17. a school break _____

18. blurred _____

Those Famous Threes

Name the famous threes below.

1. The three flavors of ice cream

   _____   _____   _____

2. The three fairies in *Sleeping Beauty*

   _____   _____   _____

3. The three fire-safety commands

   _____   _____   _____

4. The three main verb tenses

   _____   _____   _____

5. The three colors of the American flag

   _____   _____   _____

6. The three R's

   _____   _____   _____

7. The three colors on a traffic light

   _____   _____   _____

8. The three branches of the U.S. Government

   _____   _____   _____

9. The three materials the Little Pigs used to build

   _____   _____   _____

10. The three men in a tub

    _____   _____   _____

Backward and Forward

Use the clues to find the words that give a different meaning if read backwards.
An example has been done for you.

male sheep = ram (mar)

1. buddies _____

2. hit _____

3. after nine _____

4. sticky street surface _____

5. terrible _____

6. takes the skin off _____

7. shines in the sky _____

8. "_____, the Menace" _____

9. pan _____

10. victory _____

11. M.D. (slang) _____

12. prize _____

13. short sleeps _____

14. orange potato _____

15. a cutting tool _____

Compound Words

Choose a word from column **A** or **B** and combine it with a word from column **C** or **D** to make a compound word. Some words will go together in more than one combination, but there is only one combination that will use all words.

A	B		C	D
cup	handle		ball	case
foot	jelly		bar	fish
gold	over		bow	fish
high	pony		cake	light
pepper	rain		lace	mill
rail	silver		look	mint
shoe	suit		set	shirt
spot	tip		tail	toe
sun	wind		watch	ware
sweat	wrist		way	way

_____   _____

_____   _____

_____   _____

_____   _____

_____   _____

_____   _____

_____   _____

_____   _____

_____   _____

Antonyms, Synonyms, and Homophones

List whether each pair of words is made of antonyms **(A)**, synonyms **(S)**, or homophones **(H)**.

1. complex/simple _____

2. independence/liberty _____

3. dawn/sunset _____

4. colonel/kernel _____

5. empty/vacant _____

6. chute/shoot _____

7. board/bored _____

8. write/record _____

9. mix/separate _____

10. furnish/supply _____

11. fare/fair _____

12. plump/thin _____

13. over/under _____

14. job/work _____

15. air/heir _____

16. near/far _____

17. plain/fancy _____

18. beat/beet _____

19. move/transport _____

20. individual/group _____

More Antonyms, Synonyms, and Homophones

Identify each pair of words as synonyms (**S**), antonyms (**A**), or homophones (**H**).

1. _____ build-construct

2. _____ break-repair

3. _____ full-empty

4. _____ chord-cord

5. _____ dear-deer

6. _____ start-begin

7. _____ find-fined

8. _____ noise-quiet

9. _____ thanks-gratitude

10. _____ hard-soft

11. _____ guessed-guest

12. _____ vacant-empty

13. _____ flower-flour

14. _____ timid-fearful

15. _____ hoarse-horse

16. _____ tiny-small

17. _____ private-public

Palindromes

Palindromes are words, phrases, sentences, or numbers that read the same forward and backward. Write a palindrome that relates to each word or phrase below. An example has been done for you.

12 o'clock = noon

1. distress call _____

2. organ to see with _____

3. quiet _____

4. by yourselves _____

5. dad _____

6. amazing _____

7. little child _____

8. radio tracker _____

9. a joke _____

10. female parent _____

11. short for Robert _____

12. woman's name _____

13. term of respect for a woman _____

14. accomplishment _____

15. female sheep _____

Proverbs

Proverbs are old, familiar sayings that often give advice for daily living. Complete each of the following proverbs.

1. Let sleeping . . .

   _____

2. A bird in the hand . . .

   _____

3. When the cat's away . . .

   _____

4. Curiosity . . .

   _____

5. You can lead a . . .

   _____

6. The early . . .

   _____

7. Birds of a feather . . .

   _____

8. Don't count your . . .

   _____

9. You can't teach . . .

   _____

Challenge: What do all of these proverbs have in common? _____

_____

_____

_____

Similes

A simile is a figure of speech in which two unlike things are compared using the words like or as, such as in "He moved as quick as a wink." Complete the following common similes.

1. As strong as _____

2. As funny as _____

3. As hot as _____

4. As happy as _____

5. As round as _____

6. As warm as _____

7. As soft as _____

8. As silly as _____

9. As beautiful as _____

10. As red as _____

11. As loud as _____

12. As colorful as _____

13. As quiet as _____

14. As old as _____

15. As blue as _____

16. As quick as _____

17. As bright as _____

18. As heavy as _____

19. As fresh as _____

20. As smooth as _____

Country and City Match

Match the city to its country by drawing a line between them.

Cities	**Countries**
Los Angeles	*France*
Glasgow	*South Korea*
Seoul	*United States*
Bombay	*Japan*
Nagano	*Australia*
Nice	*Israel*
Frankfort	*Portugal*
Florence	*Ireland*
Toronto	*Brazil*
Lima	*Peru*
Rio de Janeiro	*Colombia*
Bogotá	*Egypt*
Lisbon	*South Africa*
Cairo	*Canada*
Jerusalem	*Scotland*
Copenhagen	*Italy*
Canberra	*Denmark*
Dublin	*Mexico*
Cape Town	*Germany*
Acapulco	*India*

Analogies

Analogies are comparisons. Complete each analogy below. An example has been done for you.

Nephew is to uncle as niece is to aunt.

1. See is to eye as _____ is to nose.

2. Ping-Pong® is to paddle as _____ is to racquet.

3. Bob is to Robert as _____ is to Elizabeth.

4. Writer is to story as poet is to _____ .

5. Car is to _____ as plane is to pilot.

6. Kennedy is to John as _____ is to George.

7. Glove is to hand as boot is to _____ .

8. Hammer is to _____ as pen is to writer.

9. Bear is to _____ as bee is to hive.

10. _____ is to picture as curtain is to window.

11. Sing is to song as _____ is to book.

12. _____ are to teeth as contact lenses are to eyes.

13. Left is to _____ as top is to bottom.

14. _____ is to pool as jog is to road.

15. Wrist is to hand as _____ is to foot.

16. Hammer is to nail as _____ is to screw.

17. Paw is to dog as _____ is to fish.

18. Meat is to beef as _____ is to apple.

19. _____ is to pig as neigh is to horse.

20. Princess is to _____ as prince is to king.

Compound Words

Write a word in the blank between each set of words. The trick is that the new word must complete a compound word both to the left and to the right of it. The first one has been done for you.

1. news   <u>paper</u>   boy

2. drop   _____   side

3. frog   _____   hood

4. foot   _____   room

5. honey   _____   light

6. water   _____   out

7. head   _____   house

8. look   _____   side

9. time   _____   spoon

10. text   _____   case

11. left   _____   board

12. birth   _____   dream

13. dark   _____   mate

14. round   _____   keep

15. butter   _____   cake

Answer Key

Page 2–Things With Numbers
1. address
2. math problem
3. price tags
4. menus
5. telephones
6. calculators
7. receipts
8. measuring cups/spoons
9. recipes
10. license plates
11. room numbers
12. pencils
13. music
14. books
15. cereal boxes
16. clothing tags
17. clock
18. watch
19. scale
20. television

Page 3–All Alike
1. types of dance
2. sports
3. flowers
4. large cats
5. desserts/sweets
6. tools
7. moods
8. gemstones
9. dairy products
10. one
11. things that are round
12. air transportation
13. writing tools
14. girls' names starting with H
15. squashes

Page 4–Word Pairs
1. huff
2. tar
3. cats
4. nook
5. thick
6. mix
7. tooth/hammer
8. cream
9. fine
10. back
11. scream
12. sticks
13. up
14. dollars
15. peaches
16. law
17. rise
18. war
19. in
20. black
21. prim
22. body/heart
23. silk
24. hook
25. pen/pencil

Page 5–Which Side Are You On?
1. side out
2. inside out
3. outside
4. four-sided
5. broadsided
6. upside down
7. bedside
8. left side
9. right side
10. sunny side up

Page 6–Car Word Parts
1. carton
2. cardinal
3. caramel
4. cardigan
5. carousel
6. cartoons
7. cart
8. carnation
9. carpet
10. carrot
11. carve
12. carnivore
13. carnival
14. carat
15. cards

Page 7–Word Pictures
1. holy cow
2. shame on you
3. one on one
4. square dance
5. paradise
6. hang on
7. hang out
8. man on the moon

Page 8–Which One Does Not Belong?
1. June–months that end in er
2. glove–footwear
3. notebook–writing tools
4. page–royalty/males
5. Rich–form of Robert
6. carnation–wood
7. layer cake–cookies
8. nephew–females
9. television–machines for talking into
10. flower–furniture
11. grapefruit–melons
12. strange–noises
13. elephant–large cats
14. lightbulb–tools
15. colon–end punctuation

Page 9–Theodore
Teddy Dalton 10
Theodore Chin 8
Ted Agee 9

Page 10–Birthday Parties
Victor–May 7
Mary–January 1
Marco–April 7
Christina–February 21
Vicky–August 3
Mike–October 30
Danielle–July 15
Peter–March 25

Page 11–What's the Question?
Answers will vary.

Page 12–Categorizing
Wood
oak
pencil
board
forest
walnut
lumber
maple
Metals
tin
iron
nail
aluminum
steel
copper
bronze
Water
bay
sea
pond
lake
river
ocean
creek
Space
countdown
Mars
moon
orbit
astronaut
weightless
rocket
Colors
tan
red
blue
green
scarlet
beige
chartreuse
Furniture
lamp
couch
mirror
chest
rocker
dresser
cabinet

Answer Key (cont.)

Page 13—How Is Your Memory?

elephant	hammer
book	key
bike	flowers
pencil	cat
hand	butterfly
pig	tree
car	

Page 14—What's the Message

1. aviator
2. England
3. pennies
4. general
5. skating
6. liberty
7. Peanuts
8. Braille
9. mission
10. authors

Page 15—Rhyming Word Pairs

1. deep sleep
2. other brother
3. can Dan
4. large barge
5. bare hare
6. tall mall
7. wild child
8. peg leg
9. dome home
10. fish dish
11. eat meat
12. silly Billy
13. fat cat
14. rude dude
15. spare fare
16. brief grief
17. more score
18. old mold
19. sad dad
20. lazy daisy

Page 16—How Many?

1. 8
2. 88
3. 500
4. 80
5. 100
6. 12
7. 6
8. 3
9. 366
10. 21
11. 18
12. 12
13. 54
14. 1,000
15. 3
16. 12
17. 10
18. 13
19. 90
20. 11

Page 17—Word Stair Puzzle

1. eat
2. tow
3. wear
4. road
5. deer
6. react
7. task
8. knife
9. egg
10. germ
11. mink
12. king
13. girl

Page 18—Double 'Em

1. essential
2. fall
3. syllable
4. vanilla
5. professor
6. sniff
7. exaggerate
8. sorrow
9. waddle
10. eyeglasses

11. footprint
12. worthless
13. macaroon
14. whinny
15. permission
16. mallard
17. recess
18. fuzzy

Page 19—Those Famous Threes

1. strawberry, vanilla, chocolate
2. Fauna, Flora, and Merriwether
3. stop, drop, and roll
4. past, present, and future
5. red, white, and blue
6. readin', 'ritin', and 'rithmetic
7. red, yellow, green
8. executive, judicial, legislative
9. straw, twigs, brick
10. butcher, baker, candlestick maker

Page 20—Backward and Forward

1. pals/slap
2. slap/pals
3. ten/net
4. tar/rat
5. evil/live
6. peels/sleep
7. star/rats
8. Dennis/sinned
9. pot/top
10. won/now
11. doc/cod
12. reward/drawer
13. naps/span
14. yam/may
15. saw/was

Page 21—Compound Words

goldfish
spotlight
sweatshirt
highway
cupcake
shoelace
railway
sunset
peppermint
football
ponytail
overlook
suitcase
jellyfish
windmill
silverware
tiptoe
rainbow
wristwatch
handlebar

Page 22—Antonyms, Synonyms, and Homophones

1. A
2. S
3. A
4. H
5. S
6. H
7. H
8. S
9. A
10. S
11. H
12. A
13. A
14. S
15. H
16. A
17. A
18. H
19. S
20. A

Answer Key (cont.)

Page 23—More Antonyms, Synonyms, and Homophones

1. S
2. A
3. A
4. H
5. H
6. S
7. H
8. A
9. S
10. A
11. H
12. S
13. H
14. S
15. H
16. S
17. A

Page 24—Palindromes

1. SOS
2. eye
3. mum
4. solos
5. pop
6. wow
7. tot
8. radar
9. gag
10. mom
11. Bob
12. Hannah/Eve
13. madam
14. deed
15. ewe

Page 25—Proverbs

1. dogs lie.
2. is worth two in the bush.
3. the mice will play.
4. killed the cat.
5. horse to water, but you can't make it drink.
6. bird catches the worm.
7. flock together.
8. chickens until they're hatched.
9. an old dog new tricks.

They are all about animals.

Page 26—Similes

1. an ox
2. a clown
3. a firecracker
4. a clam
5. a ball
6. a hug
7. a kitten
8. a clown/goose
9. a princess
10. a beet
11. a drum
12. a rainbow
13. a mouse
14. the hills
15. the sky
16. a rabbit
17. a penny
18. lead
19. a daisy
20. silk

Page 27—Country and City Match

Los Angeles–United States
Glasgow–Scotland
Seoul–South Korea
Bombay–India
Nagano–Japan
Nice–France
Frankfort–Germany
Florence–Italy
Toronto–Canada
Lima–Peru
Rio de Janeiro–Brazil
Bogotá–Colombia
Lisbon–Portugal
Cairo–Egypt
Jerusalem–Israel
Copenhagen–Denmark
Canberra–Australia
Dublin–Ireland
Cape Town–South Africa
Acapulco–Mexico

Page 28—Analogies

1. smell
2. tennis
3. Beth/Liz/Betty/Libby
4. poem
5. driver
6. Washington/Bush
7. foot
8. carpenter
9. den/cave
10. Frame
11. read
12. Braces
13. right
14. Swim
15. ankle
16. screwdriver
17. fin
18. fruit
19. Oink
20. queen

Page 29—Compound Words

1. paper
2. out
3. man
4. ball
5. moon
6. fall
7. light
8. out
9. table
10. book
11. over
12. day
13. room
14. up
15. cup